JOSEPH

ETHEL BARRETT

Regal Books

A Division of GL Publications
Ventura, California, U.S.A.

Other good Regal reading in this series:
Elijah and Elisha
Joshua
Daniel

Published by Regal Books
A Division of GL Publications
Ventura, California 93006
Printed in U.S.A.

Library of Congress Catalog Card No. 79-65232
ISBN 0-8307-0715-8

4 5 6 7 8 9 10 / 91 90 89 88

Rights for publishing this book in other languages are con-
tracted by Gospel Literature International (GLINT) foundation.
GLINT also provides technical help for the adaptation, transla-
tion, and publishing of Bible study resources and books in
scores of languages worldwide. For further information, con-
tact GLINT, Post Office Box 488, Rosemead, California,
91770, U.S.A., or the publisher.

Abraham Joseph Moses Joshua Ruth Saul David Solomon Elijah Elisha

1900 ———— 1290 ———————— 1000 ——— 925 ————— 722 ——

Exodus   Division of Kingdom

Contents

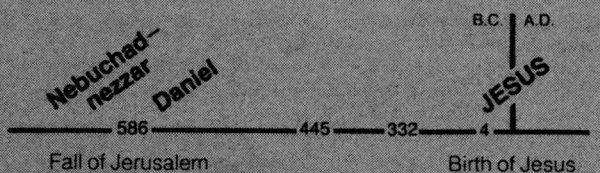

1
INGREDIENTS FOR MURDER
Genesis 37:1-3

Do you ever watch "Westerns" on television where the hero gets into so much trouble there is no way he can win—and yet you are not the least bit worried? His horse gets shot out from under him, his house gets robbed, he wanders athirst in the desert with no water in sight, his enemies threaten him—and yet you sit there without a worry, knowing that his worst problems are going to be solved and that in the end he is going to wind up victorious and happy, indeed better off than he's ever been before.

If you can say yes to this, you know right off that you're watching a *rerun*. You've seen it all before. You know exactly what's going to happen and how it's going to turn out. And there is simply no reason to worry about it or get excited. Why worry about a chap who's athirst in the desert when you know he's going to find water? Or a person beset by his enemies when you know he's going to win out? Or a person who's getting robbed when you know he's going to get it all back again?

Of course in watching a *rerun*, you may pick up some things that you missed before, or remember something you've forgotten— but there's no *tension* in it.

Life is like a rerun. *But only the part that has already happened*. We can go back in our memories and think about the things we did that we shouldn't have, or the things we didn't do that we should have. And we're a great deal wiser now because of what we have learned.

This is called 20/20 hindsight.

Now looking *ahead* is quite another matter. It's all new, and full of surprises. If we knew ahead what was going to happen, we could avoid all the mistakes and walk around all the pitfalls—there would be no need to trust God for anything for we'd know ahead of time what He was up to. Or to ask Him for anything, for we'd know ahead of time whether or not we were going to get it. And life might be easier—but the excitement would be gone.

And the wonder.

And the mystery.

In fact we'd have to come flat out and admit that life would be a bit of a bore.

With this in mind, let's get on with our story. It's a story of twelve brothers—all handsome and strong.

And loving parents.

And great wealth.

Now all of these things put together sound

like the ingredients* for a happy life. In fact all these things put together should come out very well. Of course there could be a little jealousy—even a few wingding, knock-down-drag-em-out fights. But they are hardly the ingredients for murder—

Joseph stood on the grassy slopes of the Hebron Valley in the land of Canaan. If he had to sum up his thoughts in one word, the word probably would have been "plenty." As far as his eyes could see, there were plenty of cattle and sheep and donkeys and goats, for the pastureland was good. And way off in the distance, there were plenty of olives and grapes and wheat and corn, for the soil was fertile. And plenty of huge and

*Ingredients are things to put together to make something—like the stuff your mother puts in a cake.

lavish tents for the family and servants, for his father was wealthy. The whole land was awash with plenty, for it was harvesttime. Plenty of—

"Joseph!" It was one of his brothers. He had plenty of them, too. Eleven! Actually, ten of them were half brothers, sons of his stepmother, for Joseph's real mother was dead. He had only one real honest-to-goodness "whole" brother—little Benjamin, who was hardly more than a baby.

"Jooooseph!"

Actually Joseph's half brothers could have been quite as good as whole brothers, if they'd gotten along better.

"Jooooseph!!!" It was Reuben, Joseph's oldest half brother, impatient and snurly.* "Can't you see that breakfast is ready?"

*That's halfway between sneering and surly, and it's not a good way to be.

"Coming!" Joseph cried. And he hurried toward the place where the family was gathered to eat. He ran as if he had springs in his ankles. For Joseph was seventeen, and he felt as young as the morning.

The smells of clover and grass and harvest were mixed with hot barley cakes and sweet butter and gruel. Joseph squatted in his place around the fire and looked around the circle; it was a big one. His stepmother was in the tent busy with his little brother Benjamin. The faces of his father and brothers were all crinkly and weatherbeaten and dark from the sun. His father's eyes were warm and kind and friendly. But his brothers' eyes were sullen, and their faces were snurly behind their short wiry beards. And their eyes did not look up to meet his as he reached for a barley cake.

They were angry with him and he knew it. He also knew he was no match for them, for they were older and stronger, with huge bulging muscles, while he was a slender seventeen-year-old. And his muscles?

Middle size.

And his beard?

Peach fuzz!

His brothers were grumpy enough when they weren't angry. But angry—they were downright frightening.

They had reason to be angry, for Joseph had told their father about some of the mischief they'd gotten into the night before. Mischief was their way of life. They had a talent for it. And Joseph had a talent for finding out about it. He also had a talent for reporting it to his father. This was a talent they would just as soon he would bury.

They talked to each other, ignoring him completely. They divided the chores and decided who was going to work in which pasture. When they did glance at him, they had nothing to say. But their eyes said,

Tattletale! and, *Snoop* and, *Just wait!*

Joseph scrambled to his feet first, ready to be off to do his chores.

"Wait, Joseph." It was his father. "I want to see you before you go."

His brothers started off for their day's work in twos and threes without as much as glancing at him, mumbling among themselves.

And Joseph followed his father Jacob into his spacious tent.

"I have something for you," Jacob said, and he lifted the lid of a huge carved chest and poked around inside. "I had it made especially for you."

When he found what he was looking for he held it up and shook it out to its full length. It was a coat—with many colored stripes—and beautiful!

But it was more than that. It was an *ankle*-length coat with long sleeves!

Ordinary coats came only to the knees and

had short sleeves. This was the kind of a coat that would be worn by a favorite son!

"It's the most handsome coat I've ever seen!" Joseph gasped as Jacob held it up for him to slip into. He plunged his arms into the long sleeves, hiked it up over his shoulders and felt it slither down the length of him, clear to his ankles. It was soft and beautiful.

"I never dreamed I'd ever wear anything as handsome as this," he said again, as he smoothed the folds. "This is fit for a prince! Or even a king! May I wear it today?"

Jacob chuckled. "Not in the fields," he said. "You'll be working. You may wear it tonight though, after you wash."

Joseph kept it on a few minutes longer, walking up and down and preening himself. Then he threw his arms around his father before he took it off. And with another thank you and a quick good-bye, he was off to his work, springs still in his ankles.

His job was to help some of the servants

with the grain. The men would go ahead with sickles* and whack the stalks off down by the roots. And the women gathered them up in bundles, bound them around with one of the long stalks, and propped them up straight where they stood like little people with frizzy-topped heads.

Joseph worked all day, stopping only for a lunch of cheese and bread and cool spring water. All he could think about was that beautiful coat that was waiting for him at home in his father's tent. He couldn't get his mind off it. He supposed it would cause some jealousy among his brothers. But how *much* trouble it was going to cause, he had no way of even suspecting.

*Sharp knives made of flint, with wooden handles, to cut down the grain.

2

"FATHER, I DIDN'T PLAN IT THIS WAY"
Genesis 37:4-11

A kid* was turning on a spit over an open fire and the delicious odor of it filled the air. The brothers could not see it from where they were working in the fields, but they could tell by the smoke curling up in the distance and their growling stomachs that it was time for supper.

Once home, they dived into buckets of water and gurgled and splashed until the sweat and the dirt from the day's work

*Baby goat.

were gone. Then they put on fresh robes and started for the circle around the fire. They were waiting for their father Jacob to come out and give the blessing, all jabbering happily at once—until Jacob stepped out of his tent with Joseph. And that beautiful coat. Jacob and Joseph squatted on their mats, and the brothers bowed their heads in silence while Jacob gave the blessing; they had a deep and solemn respect for their father.

"Thank you again, father," Joseph said. "It's a coat fit for a prince."

It was no way to start a happy meal.

"And you think you're one?" Simeon asked. Joseph didn't answer. And the huge meal of meat and vegetables and herbs and bread was eaten in silence for a few minutes, and then the brothers began talking among themselves as if Joseph didn't exist.

When they got ready to go their various ways for the evening, they said good-bye to their father, but their glances at Joseph said,

Tattletale and *Don't you dare*. They were
wild and they knew Joseph knew it; they also
knew that tales of their mischief always got
back to their father.

But nothing could dampen Joseph's joy
in that beautiful coat. And he folded it
carefully before he lay down on his mat for
the night. "It's fit for a prince!" was the last
thing he remembered before he drifted off to
sleep.

The days that followed were the same as
those that had gone before, but nothing
could spoil Joseph's joy in that beautiful
coat, or the princely thoughts that went with
it. And it wasn't long before the princely
thoughts got into his dreams. The dream he
had a few nights later was a strange
one—and also one he should have kept to

himself, knowing his brothers' smoldering* hatred. But instead, he could hardly wait to spill it!

He forced himself to be silent at breakfast, but at lunchtime he could keep it no longer. So while he was sitting in the fields with his brothers, munching on some fruit and bread, he spilled it all out.

"Incidentally," he said, "I had the strangest dream last night. And it was about sheaves." His brothers went on munching and gave him no encouragement. But Joseph didn't need any. "We had a lot of sheaves propped up in the field," he said. "And my sheaf was standing up straight. But your sheaves—"

They stopped munching long enough to look up at him.

"Your sheaves all gathered around mine and *bowed*. Real *low*."

*Like a fire smoking but without any flames showing.

"Ha!" Gad said. "So you want to be our king, do you?"

And, "Watch it, little brother Joe," said Levi, "before your cocky attitude gets you a smack alongside your ears."

And lunch was finished in a glum and angry silence.

Now if Joseph had quit while he was ahead, the thing might have ended right there. But he did not.

"Another dream last night," he boasted a few mornings later. "Listen to the latest. This time eleven stars—"

"Don't talk with your mouth full, Joseph," his father said softly. But Joseph plunged on.

"All these stars—and the moon—and the sun—bowed down to me. All of them."

"That does it!" Asher yelled in anger. "You just practically made an announcement that you were going to rule over us!"

It was as if the smoldering fire had burst into flames. All the brothers' eyes were blazing.

"First a princely robe," Reuben started, "which shows plainly that father prefers you before us. And now this—"

Jacob silenced him with a look. "Come now, my son," he said to Joseph. "If the stars are your brothers—are you trying to tell us that the moon and the sun are supposed to be your mother and father?* Do you think we're going to bow down to you too? The entire family? That's a bit *much*."

And nothing more was said.

Days went by, and it began to look as if the subject had been dropped.

But it hadn't been dropped.

For dreams were very important back in those days; God often spoke to people in dreams. And Jacob well knew it. And

*He meant Joseph's stepmother; his real mother was dead.

Joseph and his brothers knew it too. And so, as the days went by, nothing was said openly—

But the brothers steamed—

And Jacob wondered—

And Joseph? He went on his merry way, cheerful but, alas, still a bit cocky. He had no way of knowing the trouble and the danger that were ahead of him. Or if he had known, he wouldn't have known what to do about it. For this was not a *rerun*. He was living it for the first time. It was far from over. And only God knew what was ahead.

A few weeks later, Joseph's brothers took off with all their father's flocks to find new grazing pastures. "We're going to try up around Shechem," they told their father. "We've heard the pasture is good there."

So Jacob gave them his blessing and off they went, leaving Joseph behind.*

*And Benjamin too, of course; he was only a little boy.

Now Shechem was a town about fifty miles away and the going was slow with all those animals, so Joseph knew it would be a long time before he would see his brothers again.

At first it was peaceful. There was no quarreling or scolding, and no glowering looks.

But then it got boring. There was also no one to boast to. Things were quiet. A little *too* quiet.

Joseph began to miss his brothers. And Jacob began to *worry* about them. They could certainly get into enough mischief right around Hebron. Whatever kind of mischief could they get into way off at Shechem—and staying so long!

Finally Jacob spoke his fears aloud. "I'm concerned about them," he said to Joseph one night at supper. "I want you to go and see how the flocks and herds are doing and find out how your brothers are.

Think you can make it safely?''

"Oh, yes, father. I know I can,'' said Joseph, jumping at the chance.

"All right then,'' Jacob decided, "you'll go. We'll have provisions packed for you in the morning. You'll leave then.''

But Joseph was hardly listening. A journey like that—and completely on his own!

"Keep to the main routes,'' Jacob went on, "and don't take any side paths—they're dangerous.''

But Joseph's mind was in a whirl. He'd prove to his brothers that he could handle himself like a man. They'd teased him long enough.

"May I take my special coat?'' he asked.

"Yes,'' Jacob laughed. "You might as well go in style.''

And so Joseph started out on his long journey—a journey that turned out to be longer than he'd thought at first. For when he got to Shechem, his brothers weren't there!

And when he asked around, he learned that they'd gone on to Dothan—that was fifteen or sixteen more miles away!

The last lap of the journey was not so exciting for it had become tiresome being on his own, and he was exhausted from the long days of walking. So it was a great relief when he got to the slopes outside Dothan and saw them off in the distance.

His brothers! They actually looked *good* to him!

All his weariness left him and he began to walk faster. This surprised him. Why he was eager to see them! Why—why—

He loved them!

Astonishing!

But if he could have heard what they were talking about at that very moment, he would not have run to meet them; he would have turned on his heels and run in the other direction. For there was a battle going on among them. It was no ordinary argument. It was a battle for Joseph's very life.

3
SURPRISE JOURNEY
Genesis 37:12-30

Simeon stood in the lush valley outside
Dothan, looking over the vast expanse of his
father's sheep with a practiced eye. He could
spot trouble of any sort from miles away, for
all of Jacob's sons had been trained to do this
from their childhood. And no matter how
hot the sun or how late the day, they could
come alive and go into *Red Alert* at a
second's notice, if danger was near.
Simeon's glance swept slowly over the
landscape as it had been doing all day, when
suddenly—

He saw it way off in the distance—a bright-colored speck moving toward them.

"Well, look who's coming!" he called out to his brothers. "The master!"

And his brothers came running toward him. "Where?" they cried.

And Simeon pointed off in the distance. "Up there on the ridge," he said, "the master dreamer."

"Are you sure?"

"How can you miss that coat?"

"Oh yes—the princely coat."

"You're right, it is the master dreamer."

The brothers were huddled together now, all looking toward that bright speck in the distance. "Yes, and one day, perhaps master over *us*," Asher said, "if his crazy dreams come true." They were silent for a minute, all thinking the same thing. What if Joseph's crazy dreams *did* come true?

"Are you thinking what I'm thinking?" said Levi. They stared at him in silence.

"Go ahead, say it," he prodded. "You're thinking it. There's one sure way to see that he doesn't rule over us. We could kill him."

"No!" Reuben said quickly.

"Come on," said Dan, "go ahead and say it. You know you were thinking it too."

"We can't possibly do it," Reuben said. "Even if his crazy dreams do mean something. He's our brother."

"Our *half* brother," muttered Gad.

"It doesn't matter," Reuben said, "Even if he weren't our brother at all—whole or half—we have no right to kill him. It would be wicked. He's done us no harm. If you kill that lad, God will punish you—"

"We'll never have a better chance," Levi was saying. "Way out here, miles from nowhere—"

"God sees you," Reuben said, "no matter where you are. He sees us here too."

Now Reuben was the oldest and it was hard to talk him down. But they tried.

"Do you want that cocky brat ruling over you?" they all said at once. "Do you really? Stop and think!"

Reuben stared at all of them. His nine brothers. He saw murder in their eyes.

He looked quickly up at the ridge. The bright-colored speck was taking shape now; it *was* Joseph, and in his princely coat. Although he was still way off in the distance, his brothers could see that he was waving.

Reuben was one against nine. If they really intended to kill Joseph, it would be hard to stop them. This was going to take a little strategy. Reuben could not fight nine strong brothers. Well, then, he would have to be clever.

"Listen," he said quickly. And he pointed to an old unused well a few yards away. "We could throw him in there. There's no water in it. And there's no way he could climb back out. He'll die down there quite nicely all by himself and we can say we didn't kill him. We never even touched him."

The brothers looked at each other for a moment. And then one by one they nodded. It was agreed. The battle for Joseph's life was over.

And Joseph had lost.

Joseph's walk turned into a trot as he got closer and closer to his brothers. His feet hurt and he was tired from the long journey, but he was proud, and a little cocky too. For he had made it! He'd made the long and dangerous journey all on his own.

In the last few yards, he slowed his trot to what he hoped was a very manly stride, taking long steps. And he couldn't wipe the grin off his face.

"Father sent me," he began—and then stopped.

What he saw in their faces sent the peach-fuzz on his face aquiver and stopped him in his tracks. He had never really known until that moment how much his brothers hated him. He never finished walking those last few yards.

They came toward him.

And circled him.

Like vultures.

One by one they reached for him.

And slowly and deliberately pulled at that princely coat until they had torn it from his body.

"Watch what you're doing!" he said in a voice he hoped carried great authority. "Hold it a minute!"

They threw the coat to the ground and jerked him around. And he saw the deserted well a few yards away.

Now everything in him turned to fear.

"Master dreamer," they muttered, and, "Rule over us, will you? Well we'll see." And they dragged him toward the well, and he was kicking and screaming now.

"You can't do this!" he cried, but now he was pleading. "Help me—" He looked at Reuben. Reuben was the eldest; surely he would not let them do this. But Reuben's face was inscrutable.*

"Oh father—oh God!" Joseph cried, and now his breath was coming in short gasps. Silent now, his brothers tied a rope around him, underneath his armpits. And hiked him over the broken stones that circled the old well, to lower him down.

"God!" he said again, and now he was absolutely terrified.

"Easy now," Reuben was saying. "Easy now. Let him down easy."

Joseph was clawing at the sides of the

---

*Joseph couldn't tell *what* Reuben was thinking!

36

well. He clawed and clawed, all the way to the bottom, in vain. The last he saw of his brothers were their faces, peering down the well at him. "You rule over *us*—little Joe?" they sneered.

Then they dropped the rope and it came down writhing like a snake, and coiled around Joseph.

And then they were gone.

He called after them, frantic now. "You can't do this!" he cried. "Father—father!" Until at last he sat, all hunkered up and sobbing, his face streaked with dirt. "Father," he sobbed.

At first he was talking to his father Jacob, back home waiting for him, and maybe praying for him.

Then he found himself talking to his heavenly Father. "Lord," he said, and he hiked up his shoulder and wiped his nose on his tunic sleeve. "It's dark down here." And suddenly he seemed to feel that God was very near. "My brothers dumped me down here," he said, encouraged. "Are you going to get me out of here so I can go back to my father Jacob?" No answer. "It's dark down here," Joseph said again.

"I know, Joseph," the answer came back. "I'm down here with you."

Joseph let that spin around in his head for a few minutes. *Of course.* The Lord was everywhere, even down here at the bottom of this well. It sent Joseph's mind a-reeling. He looked up for the first time at the only little spot of sky that he could see. And he knew suddenly that no matter what happened, he was in God's hands. He'd remember that for the rest of his life.

A few yards away from the well, the princely coat lay crumpled on the ground, dirt-streaked, forgotten. The brothers were gathered around their fire eating their supper. Reuben had gone off to look for more pasture.

They ate silently, each with his own thoughts. And suddenly—

"Caravan!" Judah said, getting to his knees, then springing to his feet.

"Where?" they cried.

"Way off there. They're coming this way. On their way to Egypt, probably."

One by one they sprang to their feet. They could all see it now.

Sure enough. It was a caravan. Camels loaded with silks and spices and herbs. Traders, probably, coming from Gilead and on their way to Egypt.

Judah spoke their thought aloud. "Sell him!" he said. "We can sell him!"

They all looked toward the well where Joseph was. "Remember what Reuben said? That we should not have our brother's blood upon our hands? That God would punish us?''

They nodded.

''All right, then, sell him!'' Judah went on. ''We can sell him to these traders. Wash our hands of him.''

''Instead of killing him, we can just get him off our hands without shedding a drop of blood.''

''But what will Reuben say?''

''Reuben isn't here. So who cares?''

''Let's do it quickly. No haggling. Just let them name their price.''

And before the caravan hardly came to a stop, some of the brothers were running to meet it while the others headed for the well and started to lower a rope.

''Tie it under your arms!'' they yelled to Joseph. ''And hurry!''

In a moment they hauled Joseph up. He swayed in the air like a pendulum on a grandfather clock.

And a few minutes after that, with no haggling over price, he was being dragged off to Egypt!

His brothers had sold him as if he were a barley loaf!

What was this?

God had delivered him from the bottom of the well—

But he was on his way to Egypt—a slave! He was going in the wrong direction—He should be going back home!

What was the Lord up to?

The script was all wrong!

It should be sent back for a rewrite!

Joseph stumbled along—one merchant in front of him, one behind—and his wrist was shackled to a camel harness. There was no chance of escape.

But there was a strange hush in his heart now. "My way," the Lord seemed to be saying. "Let me work it out my way."

And the clop clop of the camels' feet in

the soft earth seemed to echo it—*My way,
My way*—

When Reuben returned, the brothers were
back at their camp fire, eating their supper as
though nothing had happened. They
watched him as he kept glancing toward the
well. Then—"No need to think of Joseph
now," they finally said. "He's not there.
He's gone."

Reuben looked at them in unbelief. "We
didn't kill him," they answered his
unspoken question. "We sold him." And
Judah held up a money pouch and jingled
twenty pieces of silver. If they expected
Reuben to be delighted, they were
disappointed.

He was *horrified*!

"You were planning to feed him?" they
asked Reuben.

"I was planning to *rescue* him," Reuben answered. "While you slept. And send him back to our father, where he belongs."

And he scrambled to his feet and looked over the horizon.

He could see nothing.

It was too late. The caravan was gone.

The only thing left of Joseph was the princely coat, crumpled in the sand.

4
"LORD, IT'S SCARY HERE"
Genesis 37:31-36

Egypt! It was unlike anything Joseph had
ever seen before. For Joseph was a country
boy, and though his father Jacob was
wealthy, his wealth was in flocks and herds
and tents. And though there were cities
throughout the land, Jacob had had very
little to do with them. But this place,
bustling with excitement! Streets filled with
people and shops filled with silks and spices
and food and jewels and dazzling things
from all over the world! Joseph's eyeballs
were on swivels as they darted from side to

side; he could scarcely take it all in.

The merchants who bought him led their caravan expertly through the busy streets of one of the greatest and most important cities in all Egypt, where the Pharaoh* lived and ruled and had his palace.

Joseph's mind was so full of questions they were stumbling over each other. But he couldn't ask any—not even one. For one thing he was not the favorite son of a wealthy man any more—he was a slave. If he had dared to open his mouth to speak at all, he would have been promptly smacked on the side of the head, and knocked into silence. Or if anyone had listened it would not have done him any good, for those all about him were speaking in Egyptian. So he wisely kept his eyes and ears open—and his mouth closed (which was a new experience for him) as he was pushed by the merchants

*That's what they called Egyptian kings.

through the streets and into what looked like a huge market square.

He was silent as he was half led and half pushed up a pair of steps to a huge platform where he stood along with dozens of other slaves, chained like himself. His tunic was torn and dirty and streaked with sweat.

"Lord," he said in his mind, "it's scary up here. I feel like little Joe again—helpless and despised by my brothers."

"Stand up straight," the Lord seemed to say. 'You are not little Joe. You are Joseph."

"But my beautiful princely robe is gone, Lord," Joseph said. "And my father Jacob is far away."

"Lift your head, Joseph. And stand up straight, as if you had your princely robe on. And remember, I am your heavenly Father."

And Joseph straightened his shoulders and lifted his head high, looking over the heads of the mob standing in front of the slave auction block.

The bids went on, and the haggling over the prices of slaves, but it sounded like so much jabbering to Joseph. Someone grabbed him from behind and jerked his head back and forced his jaw open to show his teeth. "Lord, they act as if they're selling horses or donkeys," Joseph cried in his heart. "I feel as if I should neigh or bray."

"Hold it, Joseph," the Lord said. "I know exactly what I'm doing. Even in that torn tunic you look more like a king than a slave."

And indeed Joseph did. For he was one of the finest looking lads up there. And he was one of the first ones purchased—and by a man named Potiphar.

"Lucky!" the merchants muttered gleefully as they pushed him back across the platform and down the steps toward his new owner. "Potiphar is one of the chief officials of the Pharaoh himself! He paid handsomely!" And they delivered Joseph to his new master as if he were a donkey.

Joseph might have been chained but he held his head high, and looked his new master right in the eyeballs. Then Potiphar turned on his heels, and Joseph followed him and his overseer to his home.

What a home! Joseph could hardly believe his eyes.

It was a palace! Beautiful courtyards with sparkling fountains and all kinds of flowers!

And doorways leading to spacious rooms furnished with the finest of rugs on the floors and the most expensive tapestries hanging on the walls.

A huge dining hall!

And the kitchens!

Joseph's father had always had luxurious tents—but this! He had never had anything like this! Why even the slaves' quarters were not too bad. Clearly Potiphar was an important and wealthy man!

Joseph was allowed to bathe and was given a clean tunic and new sandals. He was ready for his new life.

Back in Dothan, the brothers gathered their sheep and prepared for the long trek back to their father in Hebron. They were surly and silent. Reuben looked so woebegone* that none of the others dared to speak to him. Joseph's coat was draped over a stone, and though they didn't talk about it, it was a constant reminder of the terrible thing they had done.

Then Judah said aloud what they'd all been thinking. "There's only one thing to

*He was *miserable*.

do.'' And he picked up the coat. ''Make it look as if Joseph was killed by a wild animal. Simeon—go get a goat and kill it.'' And he began to tear the coat in several places.

When Simeon returned with the goat, they laid it on some rocks, took some of its blood and spattered it on the coat, and Judah rolled it up and stuffed it in his dufflebag. Then they started back, hardly speaking to each other during the entire journey.

Facing their father Jacob was hard to do, but the nasty business had to be gotten over with. They held the robe up before him, torn and bloody. ''We found this in a field,'' they said. ''Is it Joseph's?''

The look of shock and horror on Jacob's face was one they would not soon forget. He took the coat with trembling hands and buried his face in it and began to cry. ''Oh Joseph,'' he moaned, ''Joseph, my son, my son.'' His grief was terrible to look upon, and he would not be comforted. "I shall mourn for Joseph until I die," he said. And as the weeks dragged into months, it began to look as if he meant it.

And the brothers had to live with their guilt. They may have called Joseph a "cocky brat," but he surely was a lively and happy one and, even they had to admit, a good one.

And they could not look at Reuben without remembering what he had told them—"If you do this terrible thing, God will surely punish you."

Clearly, Joseph's absence had taken the ginger out of the entire family.

5
UP AND DOWN IN POTIPHAR'S HOUSE
Genesis 39:1-20

Potiphar was a very important man, one of the most important in Pharaoh's service. He traveled in the best circles, dined lavishly,* entertained a great deal, and indeed was a man who had no time or thought for slaves.

There was something about this new slave Joseph, however, that caught his attention. A big fellow he was, and extraordinarily handsome. In fact he was so strong and good looking that people turned to stare. But slaves had come and gone in Potiphar's

*His table was loaded with the best food!

house and many of them had been handsome.

So that wasn't it.

It was something else. It wasn't just that Joseph went quietly about his duties and did his work extremely well; it was that everything seemed to be running more smoothly in Potiphar's household since he'd come.

"Give that lad the same diet the family eats," Potiphar told the cook. "And give him more responsibility," he told his overseer.

Could it be that the Lord was with Joseph? As the weeks went by, it certainly looked as if that were so. Joseph was indeed "full of smarts."

"Let him sit in on the classes and listen to the tutors," Potiphar told his officials.*

---

*A man of Potiphar's importance would have all sorts of high-ranking officials and secretaries and managers to run his business and tutor his children.

"But the young man is so quiet and polite—he never opens his mouth," they replied. "He has nothing to say."

"I have a feeling that when he learns our language, he'll have plenty to say. And it will be worth hearing," Potiphar said. "I think he has the wisdom of God."

And it turned out to be true. For Joseph wasn't very gabby, but he prayed a lot. And before long it became obvious that he was indeed "full of smarts."

Eventually Potiphar had him running his whole household. And then his business affairs too!

Now all of this was very heady business, for you remember Joseph had been a very cocky lad. And you'd think that all of this would make him a very conceited man.

Not so.

For the more he prayed the more humble he became, until all his boyish bravura* was

*Big mouthed bragger.

gone, even though he had the highest position in Potiphar's household. He was so humble and God had blessed him with such great wisdom, that all he had to do was say *Jump,* and all those working under him would say *How high?*

And his appearance!

His tunics and his robes and his headgear got fancier and fancier. They were now made of the most expensive linens and silks and wools.

He had filled out now, too. He was not the slender lad he had been. His shoulders had broadened and his muscles had toughened and he was so strikingly handsome that everyone who looked at him turned around and looked twice—the people in the marketplace, the people who came to Potiphar's palace to do business, the people who came to pay their bills, the people who came to collect money, and Potiphar's wife—

Potiphar's wife—

She loved Joseph. And wanted him to love her too. And she told him so.

Joseph was horrified.

Why Potiphar had given him an education and trusted him with running his house and his business. Would he repay all Potiphar's kindness by stealing his *wife*?

Unthinkable.

It would be a wicked thing to do. And Joseph told her so.

And then his fine new life began to crumple. For Potiphar's wife did not know God as Joseph did. And her love turned to hate. She had nothing on her mind now but *revenge*. And what sweeter revenge could she have than to topple Joseph from his high place? Now it would take a great deal of hate to do a thing like that to an innocent person, but Potiphar's wife had plenty of hate and some to spare. So she juggled the facts around a bit and twisted them into horrible lies—and told her husband Potiphar.

"This—this—*slave*," she wept.*
"You've trusted him with your household
and your business. And now he wants to
steal your wife. He wants me to run off with
him!"

"Steal—my—wife!??!" Potiphar hissed.
And at that moment Joseph's world went
crashing about his feet.

He was seized like a common criminal.
His fine clothes were stripped from him.
And he was led away in chains. An hour
later he was in prison. Joseph was too
stupefied to fully grasp what had happened
to him.

---

*They were either crocodile tears or tears of rage.

6
WHAT'S GOD UP TO?
Genesis 39:21—40:23

"Lord, it's dark in here."

"I know, Joseph."

"But I'm not scared the way I was back in
the well."

They stayed for awhile in a long unhurried
silence, Joseph and God. For Joseph had
learned by now that praying wasn't all
talking. A lot of it was just being *quiet* and
knowing that God was there.

He looked down at his rough prison garb.

First he'd had his princely robe stripped
from him and been dumped into an old well.

This time he'd had his princely robes stripped from him and been thrown into prison. It surely was up-again-down-again with these princely robes.

But the other time he'd been cocky and bragging and very irritating to his brothers. And while that was no reason for their wanting to kill him—still he hadn't been totally blameless. But this time he was perfectly innocent. Surely God couldn't have had him thrown into prison to *punish* him.

Then, like a soft breeze, the Lord wandered into his thoughts again.

"I brought you here to bless you, Joseph."

Joseph leaned against the stone wall of the dark prison cell and sighed. A great hush and an immense peace settled over his head. "If you say it is so, then it is so, Lord," he said at last.

And then he drifted off to sleep.

And it *was* so! When Joseph was unchained and put to work among the other prisoners, he not only did his work well, but he was cheerful and patient about it. And smart, too. *Very* smart.

So smart, in fact, that the chief jailer kept his eye on him for a few weeks, and then put him in charge of the other prisoners. And it wasn't very long before Joseph was running the entire prison! And he lighted up the place! "You can't keep a good man down" might have explained it to those who were with him, but Joseph knew better. It was because God was with him.

I wish I knew what you were up to Lord, Joseph thought, but the answer always came back, "One step at a time, Joseph. Just trust me."

But, Joseph wondered, *how would God work it out*? For Joseph was there on a very serious charge; he had offended Potiphar, one of the Pharaoh's chief officials, and one who, incidentally, was in charge of all the prisons.* He could have sent the order down to have Joseph beheaded at any minute.

But another tale began to unfold and it was very strange indeed.

It began this way.

One day two new prisoners were admitted to the dungeon. And no ordinary prisoners were they! They were high officials. One was the Pharaoh's chief butler—the head of all the wine cellars—a very important man indeed in the Pharaoh's palace. The other was the Pharaoh's chief baker, in charge of all his food. And they were in there waiting for their cases to be investigated to see what was going to happen to them! And Potiphar sent the word down that Joseph was to be in charge of them.

Well, Joseph did take charge of them, cheerfully. He heard their woeful tales of

*He was captain of the guard.

64

how they had offended Pharaoh and been thrown in prison, and tried to make them as comfortable as possible.

But then the tale gets stranger still. For this mysterious business of dreams came back into Joseph's life again!*

It started one morning, when he found the baker and the butler looking very dejected.

''What in the world is the matter with you?'' he asked.

''We had dreams last night. Both of us.''

Joseph's ears pricked up.

''Mostly I can never remember my dreams,'' the chief butler said, ''I can remember only snatches of them.''

''Nor I,'' said the chief baker. ''But these dreams were different. We remember every bit of them. But there's nobody around here who can tell us what they mean.''

Joseph sat down between them and made

*Remember the dreams he'd had back in his father's house in Canaan?

himself comfortable. "Only God can tell what dreams mean," he said. "But tell me about them. Perhaps I can help you." He turned to the chief butler. "You first."

"Well," the butler began, "I saw a vine. And it had three branches. And as I looked, it began to bud, and then it blossomed, and soon there were clusters of grapes on them. Beautiful grapes. Ripe, and ready for squeezing. So I took the Pharaoh's cup in my hand. And I squeezed the grapes and filled the cup with juice. And the Pharaoh held out his hand, and I gave him the cup. And he drank the juice."

Joseph was silent for a minute. And then, "I know what the dream means," he said. "The three branches mean three days. It means that Pharaoh is going to take you out of prison and give you your position back. In three days. And when you do go back—"

"Yes?" said the chief butler.

"When you do go back, remember me.

Mention me to the Pharaoh, that I interpreted your dream. Perhaps he will let me out of here.''

The chief butler was so delighted, it was easy enough to make a promise. He could hardly believe his good fortune.

The chief baker was delighted too; he could hardly wait to find out what *his* dream meant. ''Well in my dream,'' he began, ''I had three baskets on my head. And in the top basket were all sorts of pastries and good food for the Pharaoh. But the birds came along and ate them out of the basket, and I couldn't stop them.''

''The three baskets mean three days for you also,'' Joseph said slowly. ''But your dream has no happy ending.''

The baker's crime must have been much more serious than the butler's; still it was hard to tell him that the birds pecking away at the food on his head meant that he was going to get that head lopped off. It was painful, but Joseph told him the truth.

But the tale grew even stranger.

For in three days, everything Joseph had told them came true!

It happened this way.

It was the Pharaoh's birthday. And during the great celebration, he sent to the prison for both the butler and the baker. It was a sad day for the baker, for he was sentenced to death.

It was a happy day for the butler for he was restored to his old position.

BUT—

He was so happy that he forgot everything but his own joy—*including the favor Joseph had asked of him!*

The weeks went by, and the months.

Then a year.

And Joseph wondered about it. It didn't seem to make sense.

He'd gotten the best of educations. And excellent training in how to run a house.

Then a business. And then a prison. He'd lost his cockiness. He knew how to deal with people. What *else* did he have to learn?

The answer was—*patience*! And trust.

And of course if he had known that was the answer he would not have learned either of them. Or if he had managed to learn *patience*, he would never have learned the *trust* or *faith*. For we learn these only when we don't know what's ahead. And what was ahead?

Well the story got stranger *still*.

Months dragged into a year.

Incredible! A year and a half.

Impossible!

Two years. Stupefying!

And then the story got stranger than *ever*!

7
WHO'S DREAMING NOW?
Genesis 41:1-44

It was early morning, hardly light yet, but the palace of the great Pharaoh was ablaze with light and abuzz with excitement. In the enormous kitchens below, the cooks were astir. And in the enormous upper chambers of the Pharaoh, the wise men and magicians were pacing the floor, and the Pharaoh himself was sitting on a royal couch in troubled thought.

For he had had a dream. In fact, two dreams which upset him greatly.

What? Dreams again?

Yes, dreams again.

Double dreams this time.

"Two of them," the Pharaoh moaned, holding his head in his hands and rocking back and forth. "Two of them. Can no one tell me what they mean?"

And no one could. Not one. He was surrounded by his advisors, his magicians, his chief butler—

Who suddenly stopped in his tracks.

"I forgot to tell you—I forgot to tell you, my lord!" he cried.

"Tell me what?" said the Pharaoh, raising his head and staring in surprise.

"Well, awhile back, when you put me in prison along with your chief baker—each of us had a dream. And in the prison there was a young Hebrew in charge. His name was Joseph. And we told him our dreams—" And he blurted the whole story—all of it. "—And everything this Hebrew told us came true. The baker lost his head and I was restored to my position. The Hebrew begged me to tell you about it," he ended breathlessly. "And I forgot—"

But the Pharaoh was hardly listening now. He was nodding to one of his officials. "Get Potiphar to release this Hebrew at once," he said. "And bring him to me. Quickly." The official nodded and turned on his heels and was gone before the Pharaoh had hardly gotten the words out of his mouth. "So he interprets dreams, does he?" the Pharaoh said half to himself. "Well, we'll see . . . "

Joseph was already up, bathed and dressed and about his chores when the chief jailer surprised him with the good news.

"Orders for your release," he said excitedly. "From the Pharaoh himself.

You're to be brought to him at once." And before Joseph could answer, the jailer went on, "You'll need to shave. And quickly! And here are some clean clothes."

Joseph didn't need to be told twice. He shaved and *prayed* and changed and *prayed*—

He'd spent many long unhurried hours in prayer with God. But this time he prayed "on-the-run." He asked God for wisdom as they rushed him from the prison up the steps to the street level, unbolting and bolting doors again as they went. Then—through the early morning deserted streets to the great palace of the Pharaoh!

When Joseph entered the palace, he was stunned for a moment. He'd grown used to living in riches at Potiphar's castle. But it was nothing compared to this! This was so bedazzling it sent the mind aspinning.

When he was ushered into the room where Pharaoh was, he bowed low. He had been properly trained at Potiphar's house. But when he straightened up again he looked at Pharaoh with a level gaze and without fear. For God had given Joseph something of far greater worth than money or education. And when Pharaoh looked at him, he saw a man tall and straight and handsome—but more than that. There was something about him that was noble, something powerful and mysterious. "I have heard that you can interpret dreams," the Pharaoh began without wasting any words. "That's why I sent for you."

Joseph waited.

"I had two dreams last night," the Pharaoh went on, "and none of my wise men or magicians can tell me what they mean."

"Neither can I, my lord," Joseph said quietly. "But God can."

The Pharaoh looked at Joseph in surprise for a moment. And he thought, *Could this man really have the wisdom of God?*

But aloud he said, "I dreamed two dreams. In the first one, I was standing on the bank of the Nile River. And suddenly seven cows came up out of the river and started grazing along the riverbank. The grass was green and lush, and the cows were fat and healthy looking.

"But then seven more cows came up from the river. And they were so skinny and bony and hungry looking it was pitiful. I've never seen such skinny cows in all of Egypt as those cows in my dreams.

"But then as I stood there watching, the seven skinny cows went up to the seven fat cows—and *ate* them."

No one said anything. The room was silent.

"Well," the Pharaoh went on, "I went back to sleep. But then I had another dream. It was seven again, only this time there were seven heads of grain on a stalk. And they were plump and full and healthy and ready to harvest. And then—while I stood there and watched—seven more heads of grain grew out of the stalk. Only these were thin and withered. And the thin heads swallowed up the fat ones!''

He looked at Joseph earnestly. ''This time I couldn't go back to sleep,'' he said. ''I was deeply troubled. I told my wise men and magicians all of this. And not one of them could tell me what it means. Can you?''

Now if the wise men expected any chanting or hopping up and down or any other kind of mumbo jumbo, they were disappointed.

''Both dreams mean the same thing,'' Joseph began quietly. ''The seven fat healthy cows and the seven fat heads of grain mean seven years. So your cattle will be the best Egypt has ever known—grade A milk, and grade A prime quality meat—for seven years. And your crops will be healthy and your harvest will be abundant* for seven years. BUT—"

The Pharaoh stared hard at Joseph.

Joseph's eyes never wavered. "The seven skinny cows and the seven withered heads of grain also mean seven years," he said. "And they mean famine. Your crops will fail and your cattle will be sickly for lack of food. And there will be a great famine in the land—for seven years.

"So there will be seven years of plenty— followed by seven years of famine."

Joseph waited for Pharaoh to grasp this, then, "Now God has said this is going to happen, and soon," he said. "And He gave you this double dream to let you know He means it."

It was a bombshell. But before the Pharaoh could recover and find his voice,

*Super big.

Joseph went on. "This is what you must do," he said earnestly. "Appoint officials to collect one-fifth of all the crops, and put them in royal storehouses to keep until the seven years of famine come. Now this is a big undertaking, and to make sure the whole project doesn't get bogged down in red tape and governmental gobbledygook, put one man in charge of the whole thing—the wisest man you can find in all of Egypt."

The wisest man in all of Egypt?

The Pharaoh and his officials got into a deep discussion about it, and Joseph stood by, straight and tall—and silent. His mind went back to when he was a lad of seventeen, bragging in front of his father and his brothers. He thought of the long trek into Egypt, the years in Potiphar's palace, the years in prison. How long had it been? Twelve years? Thirteen years? Why he was thirty years old now!

Exactly *what* had God been preparing him for?

And at the very moment Joseph was asking himself this, Pharaoh was saying to his officials, "Who could undertake a project as big as this better than this man Joseph himself? We have plenty of educated and trained politicians about—but this man has the wisdom of God."

And the next moment Pharaoh turned to face Joseph with the astounding news, "You recommend that we find the wisest man in the country," he said, "and we believe we have found him. The man is you."

There was a moment of agreement throughout the big room. Then Pharaoh took off his signet ring* and placed it solemnly on Joseph's finger. "I hereby appoint you, Joseph, to be in charge of this great project," he said. "Next to me you will be the highest authority in all of Egypt."

*A token of the highest authority! Wow!

Next, a royal golden chain was placed about Joseph's neck.

Then a beautiful robe was placed about his shoulders.

And after much rejoicing, he was led to a suite of royal chambers. "Just temporary," they explained, "until we can prepare you a place of your own."

Joseph never went back to prison again.

8
OLD DREAM REVISITED
Genesis 41:45—43:15

Prime minister of Egypt!

Joseph had gone from the princely coat
his father had given him to the clothing of a
slave.

Then from the coat he'd worn in
Potiphar's palace to the clothing of a
prisoner.

And now he was in a princely coat again.
And what a coat this time! For now he was
wearing royal clothing, reserved only for
Egypt's mighty men, with the chain of

royalty and authority around his neck, and the signet ring of the Pharaoh himself on his finger.

And that wasn't all. He rode in the finest of chariots through the city streets with officials running before him crying to the people, "Pay attention! Bow the knee!"

And to add to all this, the Pharaoh gave him a fine palace of his own. And a noble woman for a wife!

Wow!

Joseph had prayed from many places during his life.

From the old well, and the prison—*Lord, it's dark in here*.

And from the auction block in the slave market—*Lord, it's scary up here*.

And now he had zoomed to the very top. But he still had long unhurried talks with God. For these were lofty heights that could go to your head—maybe even make you cocky again.

"Lord, it's awfully high up here."

"I know, Joseph."

"Enough to make me dizzy."

"Yes."

"Stay with me, Lord, I pray you, and keep on giving me wisdom. And please Lord—don't ever let me be cocky or let all this go to my head."

And so they talked together, Joseph and God.

Well it *was* pretty heady business.

And Joseph needed God more than he'd ever needed Him before.

So his new life started.

For seven years, Egypt had bumper crops and great prosperity. And Joseph traveled all over the country supervising the storing of grain in all the cities, until the granaries were so full they were ready to burst. And everywhere he went, people bowed as his chariot went by.

Seven years.

And then the great test came that would tell whether or not God really had been speaking through Joseph back in Pharaoh's palace those many years ago. Would the famine come as he had predicted?

It did.

Right on the nose.

No rain.

No harvest.

No pastureland for the flocks and herds.

Withered heads of grain and skinny cattle, just as the Pharaoh had seen in his double dream.

It all came true.

Joseph put the other half of his gigantic plan into operation. The huge storage granaries were open, and bit by bit the grain was doled out—very carefully, so it would last the full seven years.

The famine had spread far and wide, even to other countries. And people came from everywhere to buy grain, for they were starving too. It took a great and mighty man to rule over all this business and see that it was done properly. And Joseph was the man for the job. There was not a man in all of Egypt as mighty as he.

And then something shot back into his life and hit him broadside and sent his head spinning. It was a memory of an old old dream. And it happened this way.

He was sitting in his lofty chair as if it were a throne, elevated on a platform, surrounded by officials of every description ready to do his bidding at a snap of his fingers. For all the people who had come from foreign countries to get permission to buy grain—had to deal with Joseph first.

They came in ones and twos, and larger groups also—every color and description, all begging for permission to buy grain.

It was one group of ten men that sent the old dream careening back into Joseph's life. They came up to the bottom step of the platform on which Joseph was seated and bowed low, their faces to the ground. And all the years seemed to wash away like footprints on beach sand wash away when the tide goes out.

They were his brothers!

Just as he had dreamed that the eleven sheaves and the eleven stars would bow down to him—his brothers were hitting the dirt!

Though all Joseph's insides were twitching with surprise, the long years of suffering had taught him great self-control. So his face was impassive* when he spoke to them.

''Where are you from?''he demanded.

They looked up at him. Strong, sly, brave, foxy, cruel, jealous—they had been all of these things. Were they still? Could he trust them now? They had to be tested.

*Calm, cool and collected.

"You're spies!" he said. "You've come to see if there are any weak places in our border defenses."

"Oh no!" they cried, all speaking at once. "We've come to buy grain! We're honest men. From Canaan! We're all brothers!"

"You are spies," Joseph insisted.

"Sir," they said, desperate now, "there are twelve of us. Our father is back in Canaan. And our youngest brother—he's home with our father. And one of our brothers is dead."

"So?" Joseph said. "That doesn't prove anything. You could still be spies." Outside he was stern and frightening. But inside, he had a knot in his stomach. His father was still alive! And his beloved brother Benjamin was safely home! "Get up on your feet," he said. "Your story will be tested."

"But we are here—"

"Yes," Joseph interrupted, "here you

are. And here you'll stay—until one of you goes back to Canaan and brings back this younger brother you say you have. You can all think about it—in jail.'' And he signaled to one of his officials. ''Jail,'' he ordered. ''All of them.''

And jail it was—for three whole days.

Now Joseph could have had them all killed and sent for his father and his brother Benjamin to come to Egypt and live in style. After all, those rascals standing here had tried to kill *him*. But Joseph had not gone through all his suffering and all those long talks with God for nothing. So it's hardly likely that such an idea even crossed his mind. Instead he let them cool their heels in jail for three days.

At the end of three days he faced his brothers again. He stared at them, long and hard. Though they were older, they looked the same to him—except for one thing. They were absolutely scared to death.

Of course there was no way they could possibly recognize him. He was not only older, but he was dressed in the robe of a prime minister, wore the chain and signet ring of the Pharaoh—and spoke to them through an interpreter in perfect Egyptian. To them he was a foreign nobleman who didn't even speak their language. How could they know that this powerful man glowering at them not only understood every word they said, but was a Hebrew like them, and their very own brother!

"I'm going to give you a chance to prove that you are honorable men," he said. "You may go home to your families—but I'll keep one of you here as a hostage until you bring back to me your youngest brother. When you do that, I'll release the hostage—and spare you all."

They agreed eagerly, through the interpreter. Then they turned to each other and began to all talk at once. "You know why all this is happening, don't you? God is punishing us for what we did to Joseph.''

"I told you not to do it," Reuben said. "Didn't I tell you? But you wouldn't listen—no, you wouldn't listen. He probably died because of us. And now we're probably going to die, too."

And all this in front of Joseph, who could understand every word they said.

He stood it as long as he could, then turned on his heels and went into a side room. And put his face in his hands, and his tears trickled through his fingers. They no longer seemed like the cruel brothers he remembered. They were just very frightened men.

When he could control himself, he went back—the stern and powerful prime minister again. "You!" he commanded, pointing at Simeon, and beckoned some officials to put poor Simeon back in chains. He looked at the rest of them sternly.

"Begone," he said. "You're dismissed. Follow these officers. You can pay them and they'll give you your grain. Now off with you."

Then he called one of his men back. "Take their money," he said. "Let them think they're paying for their grain. But when you pack their grain, put each man's money back in the top of his grain sack." He nodded and left to obey Joseph's command.

If Joseph had intended to frighten his brothers, he had most certainly succeeded. For when they stopped on their journey home to make camp and feed their donkeys, the first one to open his sack of grain found his money in it. "We've been framed!" he gasped. "He'll say I stole it!"

This sent them all atrembling, and by the

time they got back to their father Jacob, they were paralyzed with fear.

Jacob saw them coming. First he saw the welcome sacks of grain. And then he saw their faces. "You had a bad time?" he asked.

"Worse than that," they answered. "The prime minister thought we were spies."

"Spies?" Jacob's eyes boggled. "Spies?"

"Yes! We told them we were brothers and that our youngest brother was back in Canaan with you, Father. But he wouldn't believe us."

"Wouldn't believe—"

"No! He made us leave Simeon there for a hostage!"

Jacob did a quick nose count. They were telling the truth; Simeon was missing! He sat back on a sack of grain and began to weep.

Reuben put his hand on old Jacob's

shoulder. "He told us we had to bring our youngest brother back, Father," he said softly, "to prove that we are telling the truth. It's the only way we can buy more grain when we need it." And they began to open the other grain sacks.

"NO!" Jacob cried. "Not Benjamin! You can't take Benjamin away!"

"Father!" Reuben cried, "don't carry on like that! I'll bring Benjamin back. I'll be responsible for him. You can kill my two sons if I don't bring him back safely."

"NO!" Jacob cried again. But his cries were suddenly drowned out by the cries of the other brothers who had dumped their sacks of grain out. "We've *all* been framed!" they wailed. "They've put all our money back in our sacks! They'll say we stole it and we'll never be able to prove we didn't!"

Poor old Jacob stared at the open sacks of grain and the money on top.

And he summed it all up.

"Joseph never came back home," he said, "only his bloody coat. Simeon is gone. And you've all been framed. And now you want to take Benjamin away. No." And his face grew desolate, and he began to wail with them. "Joseph is dead. And I will not lose Benjamin too!"

And then all their wailing died down into silence, each man with his own thoughts.

Jacob knew he could never let Benjamin go.

Benjamin knew they could never get Simeon back unless he *did* go.

And the other brothers knew they'd be accused of stealing if they *dared* to go.

And every last one of them was numb with terror. They did not want to even talk about it.

It wasn't until their grain was finally gone, and their stomachs were empty and growling with hunger, that the subject came up again. Old Jacob said aloud what they had all been thinking for days. "We've got balm and spices and myrrh, but we can't eat them. We must have grain," he said. "And the only place to get it is in Egypt. If you don't go back we'll all starve. And your wives and children."

"Father," Judah tried to reason softly, for he didn't want to start another wailing session, "you know we can't go unless we take Benjamin with us. That prime minister meant every word he said. And he said, 'Don't come back unless your brother is with you.' "

Jacob put his head in his hands. "Why did you tell him you had another brother?"

"Because he asked," they all said at once. "He asked us if our father was living and if we had another brother and we told him. How did we know he was going to ask us to bring our brother back?" And the old argument started all over again.

"Wait!" Judah said finally. "Send Benjamin with me, Father. I'll absolutely guarantee that he'll come back to you."

Old Jacob sighed and turned away to hide his tears. "Take double the money with you, and pack all the balm and spices and myrrh that the donkeys will carry—as gifts for this prime minister."

And so the long trek back to Egypt began *again*.

9
LUNCH WITH THE PRIME MINISTER
Genesis 43:16-34

It was what Joseph had been waiting for. He was counting the days until his brothers returned, for his plans were not yet completed.

When he saw them coming, he did a quick nose count. Benjamin was with them!

They all stood before him at last, weary from their journey. He saw nothing but anxiety and fear in their faces. But he had to carry his test through to the end. Had his brothers really changed, or were they the same rascals they'd always been?

"These men will eat with me this noon," he said, turning to the manager of his household. "Take them to my palace. Give orders for a feast."

He expected them to be frightened and as they were led away, he could see that they were.

"It's a trap," they whispered to each other, "and he's getting ready to spring it. He'll accuse us of stealing and make us all stay here as slaves!"

When they got to the palace they tried to explain themselves to Joseph's household manager. They blurted out how they'd found the money in their sacks, and that they had brought additional money to pay it back.

And to their amazement the manager told them to forget it! "Your God must have put it there," he said. "We collected your money alright."

And then he had Simeon released and brought out to them. And they were all given water for washing and told to make ready to eat.

By this time their emotions were on a yo-yo.

When Joseph arrived at his palace he found them all there, washed and refreshed, and their donkeys unpacked and their gifts spread out.

Joseph's feelings were on a yo-yo too. The strain of keeping his secret was beginning to tell on him. He looked at their gifts and thanked them, and then had to hold back his tears as they bowed low before him again.

"How have you been getting along?" he asked. "And your father—is he well?" He looked away quickly to swallow the lump in his throat, then looked back at Benjamin. "And this is the young brother you told me about?"

Benjamin looked back at him, his gaze level and honest. What a fine young man he was! "And how are you, lad?" Joseph asked. "God be gracious to you."

He wanted to throw his arms around Benjamin's shoulders and hold him close, as men did in those days.* But instead he turned on his heels and hastened from the room. It made him look like a rude fellow. But actually he tore off to his bed chamber.

And leaned against a marble pillar.

And cried.

When he could pull himself together, he washed his face and went back to the banquet room, looking every bit the stern prime minister again. He signaled that it was time to eat and where the brothers were to sit. "You," he said, looking at Reuben, "there. And you—" pointing to Simeon—"there." Then Levi. Then Judah. And so on down the line. Each brother was seated according to his age—just as if

*And still do today in those lands.

Joseph knew them! They cast each other secret glances of amazement. This ruler was something *else*. He was a powerful and frightening man. But was he also a *wizard*?

The Egyptians who were there were seated at a table by themselves. And the great prime minister sat at his own special private table, elevated on a platform above all the others.

The food was served from the prime minister's own table. And the largest servings were given to Benjamin—five times as much as the others!

As the meal progressed, everyone began to relax.

They talked.

Then they laughed.

And then they bantered back and forth until things were actually jolly!

Joseph looked at his brothers in amazement. Were these the same snurly brothers who sat around the campfire back in

Canaan, never speaking to him except to growl? How tenderly they looked at Benjamin, and with what concern! They did not look as if they wanted to toss *him* out—rather, as if they wanted to *protect* him!

Joseph got a lump in his throat just looking at them. But he couldn't reveal himself yet; the test was not over.

In fact, the most severe part of it was still to come!

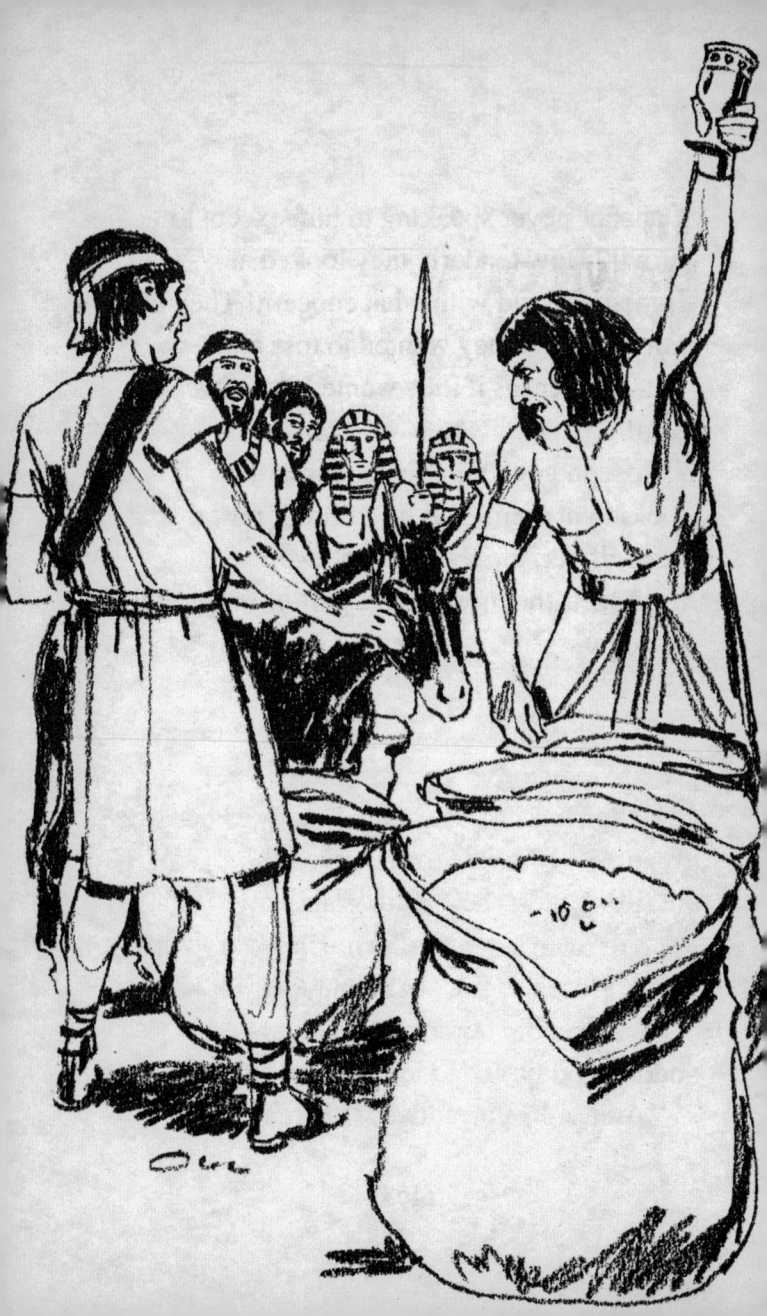

10
DAWN OF A
NEW DAY
Genesis 44:1—46:30

It was not quite dawn. The brothers were up, getting ready to go back home.

"The Hebrews are getting ready to leave, my lord," Joseph's overseer told him. "We are filling their sacks with grain now."

"Fill them to the top, as much as they will hold," Joseph said, "And put their money back as you did before." The overseer nodded and turned to leave the room.

"And," Joseph added, "there is

something else I want in Benjamin's sack—my private drinking cup, along with his grain money.''

Joseph's private silver drinking cup?

What in the world was he up to now?

The overseer nodded and left to do as he was told.

One did not question the great prime minister!

Before the sun was hardly up, the brothers left on their long journey back to Canaan, never suspecting what was in their grain sacks.

Joseph waited until they had left. Then when they were barely out of the city, he called his overseer again. ''Go after them and stop them,'' he said. ''And ask them why they have done this terrible thing after the prime minister has been so kind to them. Stealing, of all things, his personal silver drinking cup!''

The overseer went to do as he was told.

By this time he must have thought the prime minister was a little weird.

The brothers had left the city and were out on the road, their donkeys clopping along, sacks full. They were laughing and talking—what a great time they'd had!

And then they looked back and saw the prime minister's overseer coming in the distance.

Their hearts sank.

It was like driving happily along the road and then seeing the flashing red light of a police officer signaling you to pull over. And you pull over, wondering what in the world you've done wrong!

Then the chariot ground to a halt in a cloud of dust, and the overseer leaped out. *What have we done now?* they all thought, but he did not give them a chance to say it.

He said it instead. "What have you done *now*?!!?"

They just stared, their eyes boggling, their beards wobbling, and their mouths hanging open.

So he told them what they had done, that the prime minister's cup had been stolen and they were all suspects.

Then they all found their voices at once. "What kind of people do you think we are?" they babbled, and, "Didn't we bring back the money we found in our sacks?" and, "Why would we steal from your master's house?"

And then they blurted out the dumbest of all things—they should have known better—

"ALL RIGHT! Search our sacks! If you find that silver cup in any of our sacks—let the one in whose sack it is—DIE! And the rest of us will be your master's slaves—forever!"

OH FOLLY!

But the overseer said, "No. No one will die. The one who stole it will be my master's slave. The rest of you may go on home."

Wearily, they slung their sacks off their donkeys' backs and to the ground. And, starting with Reuben, began to open them, from Reuben on down.

When Benjamin's sack was opened and they saw the silver cup gleaming there in the grain, the brothers went berserk. Not with anger—but with despair.

They wailed and moaned and tore at their clothes and raised their faces to the sky.

Calamity of calamities.

Of all the things that had happened to them in all their lives—this was the worst!

Benjamin, of all people—*Benjamin*!

They tied up their sacks.

And loaded their donkeys.

And dragged their feet all the way back to the palace of the prime minister.

Joseph waited, pacing the floor. This was the final test. Everything he had been doing to his brothers led up to this point. What would happen? Which way would it go? His heart almost stopped when he saw them coming. His brothers—who had been willing to kill *him*, willing to sell him as a slave—what would they do with *Benjamin*?

He braced himself for the worst as they were led up to him.

They bowed to the ground, but he hardly waited for their faces to come up before he said sternly, "What do you think you are doing? Did you think you could get away with a thing like that? Didn't you know that a man as powerful as I am would find out who stole my silver cup?"

Judah raised his face first. "We've all returned to be your slaves," he said, "along with Benjamin. The cup was found in his sack. We—"

"No," Joseph interrupted. "He alone

stays. If the cup was found in his sack, then he's the one who will stay and be my slave. The rest of you are free. Now go!''

This was the moment.

This was it.

What would they do with Benjamin?

There was a silence.

Then Judah stepped forward, his hands outstretched, his face pleading. ''I know you could wipe us all out with a snap of your fingers,'' he said, ''but I beg you to be patient with me. Let me say just this one word to you. Hear me out, I pray you.''

Joseph nodded, waiting.

''My lord,'' Judah began, ''we have at home a father, an old man. We had another young brother. And he went away. And never returned. He is dead and our father nearly died of sorrow also, for he loved this son very much. Now this lad here—'' and he gestured toward Benjamin—''is the only young brother we have left. And our father loves him more than any of the rest of us. If we don't bring him back safely, our father will surely die of grief this time."

Joseph's insides were knotted up so he could hardly breathe, but he motioned for Judah to go on.

"I beg you, my lord, let me stay here in his place," Judah begged. "Just let my youngest brother return to his father. For how can I go back if he is not with me? I'll be your slave forever. Just let Benjamin go free."

Joseph swallowed hard and looked at his brother Judah.

This was *Judah*?

Judah, the very one who had once been willing to sell *him*, Joseph?

Hardhearted, pigheaded Judah? How the years had changed him!

Joseph could stand it no longer. He clapped his hands—"Out, out, all of you—everyone leave except these

Hebrews. Clear the room!'' he cried.

His overseer bustled everyone along and they went out, murmuring to each other, until every last one of them was gone and Joseph was alone at last with his brothers.

Joseph could not hold back his tears now; he did not even try. He sobbed aloud, his hands outstretched toward them. ''Look at me,'' he said, ''don't you know me?''

They stared at him in amazement, not knowing what to do.

''I am Joseph—''

But they could not answer. Their faces were sagging, absolutely stunned with amazement.

''I'm your brother whom you sold as a slave.''

They couldn't believe it! This handsome man with the stern face, who absolutely radiated* wealth and power? This man who,

*It shone from him like a light.

with a snap of his fingers, could have them all killed? This man they'd been bowing down to—bowing down to—*bowing down to*—

The dream!

The dream!

It had all come true! Joseph was ruler of all Egypt! He had the power of life and death over them!

The expressions on their faces turned from amazement and unbelief—to fear.

"Don't be angry with yourselves," Joseph said quickly, "and don't be afraid. For you did not do this to me, believe me. God did this to me. And you did not send me here. God sent me here. He prepared all this, each step of the way. And made me a great ruler so that I could take care of you and your families—and my father—and keep you alive."

Now they began to cry too.

"There will be more years of famine," he

said, "five more years. But God sent me ahead to prepare the way so that you would not suffer—you or your children."

They cried the harder.

"Go home and tell them now," he said. "And tell them to pack and come back here. I'll prepare a place for them where they'll be safe. Bring all your flocks and herds. For God wants you to grow and to prosper, yes, and become a great nation. Tell my father of my power here in Egypt. And oh, bring him back here to me quickly!"

They all cried again—but this time with joy!

And Joseph did at last what he'd been longing to do ever since he'd first seen his brothers. He threw his arms around Benjamin and they both cried together. Then he did the same with all the rest of his brothers—those snurly brothers—and all the fear and all the hatred and all the jealousy were washed away in their tears.

Then he sent them back to Canaan—but this time in style!

They had wagons and provisions and gifts and new clothes.* And there were ten extra donkeys loaded with goodies from Egypt, especially for Joseph's father.

When Joseph waved good-bye to them this time, they were all talking and laughing at once. "See that you don't quarrel along the way," Joseph said, and this time they all *grinned*. There wasn't a snurl in the bunch!

Well, Joseph went back to work,** but one part of his mind was always on his brothers.

---

*Benjamin got extra again; five changes of clothing and 300 pieces of silver!
**Actually, when you get to be that powerful you appoint others to do the work; what *you* need is WISDOM!

And his father? Why, every beat of Joseph's heart cried out *father, father, father*. The days went by slowly as he counted every hour. And then—

The word arrived that one of his brothers was at the palace to see him! Joseph's muscles squinched up in knots. Was something wrong? He didn't wait to have his brother shown in, but rushed out to meet him.

It was Judah. But he sighed with relief when he saw Judah's face, and before he could ask, Judah told him—and all in one breath!

"Everything is all right, Joseph! Father is all right too. He sent me on ahead to tell you so you wouldn't worry. He's beside himself with joy. He just can't bring himself to really believe it, he has to see you with his own eyes! They should all be here before the end of the day. They—"

"I can't wait!" Joseph cried. And he

clapped his hands and ordered his chariot. He sped out to greet his father as if he were on wings! It seemed that all his life pointed to this joyous moment!

As he sped along, his driver urging the horses on—faster, faster—the very chariot wheels seemed to be singing, *father, father, father*. And as Joseph sped along, his thoughts were speeding too. It seemed as if he were seeing a rerun of his life—

The clothes—the princely coat his father had given him, the handsome clothes he'd worn at Potiphar's house, the royal robes he was wearing now—all symbols of power. And the dreams—the dreams he'd had as a boy, the dreams of the butler and baker that had called Pharaoh's attention to Joseph, and then the dreams of the Pharaoh himself.

Why, everything that had happened to him—the good and the bad—had been planned by God. How perfectly all the pieces fit together! How marvelous God was! How wonderful! And he worshiped God as he sped along, his heart crying *father, father*—

And then he saw their caravan in the distance. His driver urged the horses on even faster. And they sped toward each other, Jacob and his family—lumbering along in their wagons—

And Joseph, the great ruler of Egypt, in his beautiful chariot, the wheels scarcely touching the ground!

And at last they met, and before Joseph's chariot even stopped, he leaped out and ran toward his father. And he half helped, half lifted him out of his wagon.

"Oh Joseph, Joseph, my son, my son," old Jacob said. "Now I can die happy—my Joseph is alive!"

And the frail old man, and the great ruler to whom he had once given a princely coat, cried in each other's arms.

The caravan of Hebrews went on toward Egypt. The sun cast long shadows to the side of the wagons and donkeys, making the wagons look tall, and the donkeys' legs look impossibly long. It was late afternoon.

But morning was breaking in their hearts. It was like the dawn of a new day . . .

DICTIONARY

balm.   Gum or resin which could soothe irritation and act as a mild antiseptic. It is not known for sure from what plant balm was taken.

caravan.   A group of people traveling together for long distances, usually selling and buying goods. In Bible times they used camels and donkeys to travel.

famine.   A time when there is no food for people or animals to eat. Often a famine is caused by a lack of rain. Sometimes insects, like grasshoppers, destroy crops.

gruel. The soup from grain or beans that have been boiled in milk or water.

Hebrews. The name of God's chosen people. They were also called the Israelites.

myrrh. The sap of a low bushy tree, used to make anointing oil smell good (Exodus 30:23-33), as a perfume (Song of Solomon 5:13), as a pain killer (Mark 15:23), and to prepare a body for burial (John 19:39).

overseer. One who is in charge of a group of workers.

pharaoh, Pharaoh. Not a name but the title given to the kings in ancient Egypt. An Egyptian would say ''Pharaoh Neco'' but an American would say ''President Neco.''

sheaf, sheaves.   At harvest time farmers cut the grain in stalks and tied the stalks in bundles, called sheaves.

sickles.   A curved blade with a short handle that farmers used to cut the stalks of wheat or barley.